# TABLE OF CONTENTS

D1202302

# CHAPTER 1

## WELCOME TO ICELAND!

iceberg

What country is just below the **Arctic Circle**? Iceland! This island is surrounded by water. Polar bears can be spotted on icebergs!

# ALL AROUND THE WORLD
# ICELAND

by Kristine Spanier, MLIS

pogo

# Ideas for Parents and Teachers

Pogo Books let children practice reading informational text while introducing them to nonfiction features such as headings, labels, sidebars, maps, and diagrams, as well as a table of contents, glossary, and index.

Carefully leveled text with a strong photo match offers early fluent readers the support they need to succeed.

## Before Reading

- "Walk" through the book and point out the various nonfiction features. Ask the student what purpose each feature serves.
- Look at the glossary together. Read and discuss the words.

## Read the Book

- Have the child read the book independently.
- Invite him or her to list questions that arise from reading.

## After Reading

- Discuss the child's questions. Talk about how he or she might find answers to those questions.
- Prompt the child to think more. Ask: Iceland is filled with volcanoes and glaciers. What natural landforms are found where you live?

Pogo Books are published by Jump!
5357 Penn Avenue South
Minneapolis, MN 55419
www.jumplibrary.com

Copyright © 2021 Jump!
International copyright reserved in all countries.
No part of this book may be reproduced in any form without written permission from the publisher.

Library of Congress Cataloging-in-Publication Data

Names: Spanier, Kristine, author.
Title: Iceland / by Kristine Spanier.
Description: Minneapolis, Minnesota: Pogo Books, [2021]
Series: All around the world | Includes index.
Audience: Ages 7-10 | Audience: Grades 2-3
Identifiers: LCCN 2019039925 (print)
LCCN 2019039926 (ebook)
ISBN 9781645273356 (hardcover)
ISBN 9781645273363 (paperback)
ISBN 9781645273370 (ebook)
Subjects: LCSH: Iceland—Juvenile literature.
Classification: LCC DL305 .S67 2021 (print)
LCC DL305 (ebook) | DDC 949.12—dc23
LC record available at https://lccn.loc.gov/2019039925
LC ebook record available at https://lccn.loc.gov/2019039926

Editor: Jenna Gleisner
Designer: Molly Ballanger

Photo Credits: Andrew Mayovskyy/Shutterstock, cover; Juniors/SuperStock, 1; Pixfiction/Shutterstock, 3; Andrew Peacock/iStock, 4; Mauritius/SuperStock, 5; Getty, 6-7; Alex Alferez/Shutterstock, 8; Arctic Images/Alamy, 9; mantaphoto/iStock, 10-11; digital_eye/iStock, 12-13; grintan/Shutterstock, 13; Timmethy/Shutterstock, 14l; Whiteaster/Shutterstock, 14r; Image Source/iStock, 15; patpongs/iStock, 16-17; Christian Science Monitor/Getty, 18-19; Mlenny/iStock, 20-21; johan10/iStock, 23.

Printed in the United States of America at Corporate Graphics in North Mankato, Minnesota.

reindeer

The Arctic fox was once the only wild animal here. Visitors to the island brought reindeer. Mink, rats, mice, and rabbits are now here, too.

Do you want to whale watch? You could spot humpback whales! Orca whales, pilot whales, and blue whales swim in the seas. Salmon, trout, and cod are also here. Fish are an **export**.

## WHAT DO YOU THINK?

Iceland has a strict fishing law. People from other countries can't fish within 200 miles (322 kilometers) of Iceland's shores. Do you think this is fair? Should countries be able to control the oceans? Why or why not?

humpback
whale

# CHAPTER 2
# LAND OF FIRE AND ICE

Hekla

Iceland is known as the land of fire and ice. Why? It has **glaciers**. But it also has around 200 **volcanoes**! Hekla is the most **active**. It is 4,892 feet (1,491 meters) high.

Surtsey

Surtsey is an island 20 miles (32 km) from the south coast. It was created by volcanic eruptions. They began in 1963. They lasted four years. People do not live on this island.

Vatna Glacier is here. It is the largest glacier in all of Europe. It covers about 3,200 square miles (8,288 square km). This is almost as big as the country of Puerto Rico!

## DID YOU KNOW?

Iceland is considered part of Scandinavia. This is an area of countries in Europe. It also includes Sweden, Norway, Denmark, and Finland.

Vatna Glacier

Much of the land here is rocky. It is difficult to farm. Sheep, cattle, and horses feed in **meadows** near the sea. Sheep wool is used to make sweaters.

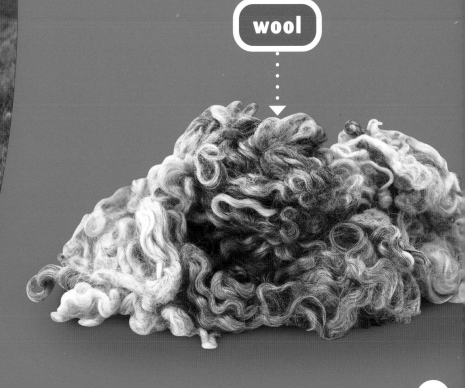

wool

# CHAPTER 3

# ICELAND'S PEOPLE

Many meals here include lamb or fish. Gravlax is salmon cured with salt. It is flavored with dill. People also enjoy skyr. It is like yogurt. It is eaten with bilberries.

bilberries

gravlax

skyr

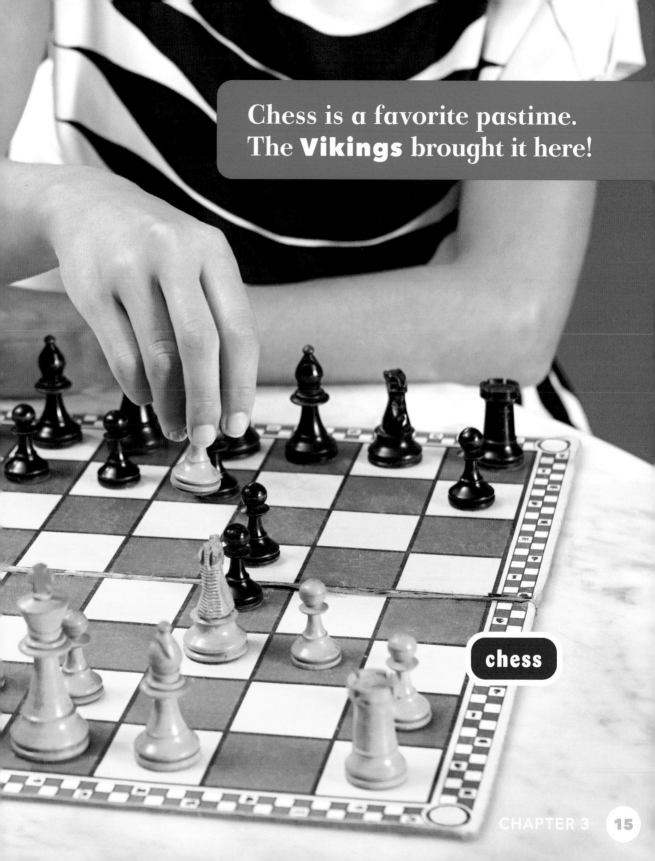

Chess is a favorite pastime. The **Vikings** brought it here!

chess

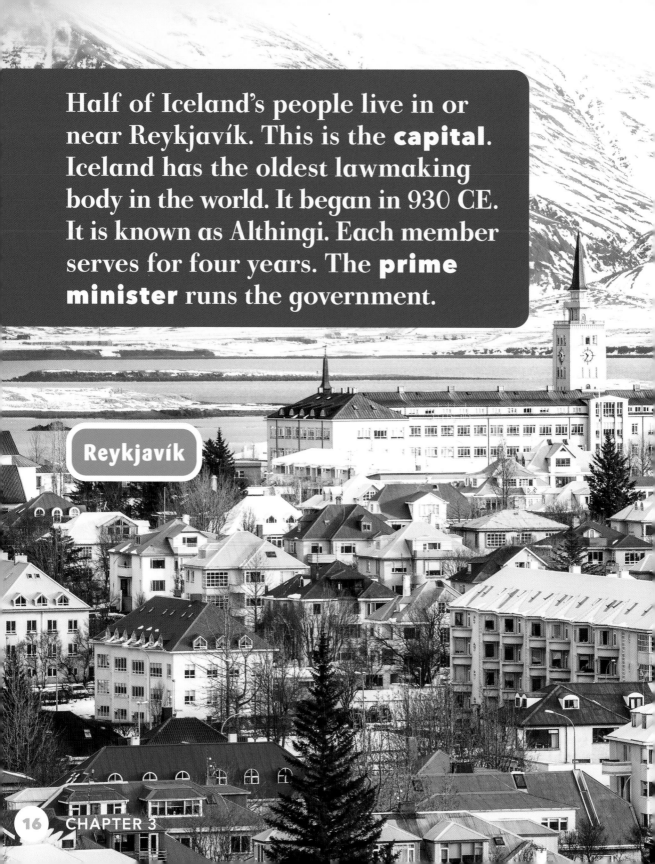

Half of Iceland's people live in or near Reykjavík. This is the **capital**. Iceland has the oldest lawmaking body in the world. It began in 930 CE. It is known as Althingi. Each member serves for four years. The **prime minister** runs the government.

Reykjavík

# TAKE A LOOK!

Iceland's flag has important meanings. What are they? Take a look!

◼ = fire from Iceland's volcanoes
◻ = snow and ice fields
◼ = sea
✛ cross = shows **unity** with other Scandinavian countries

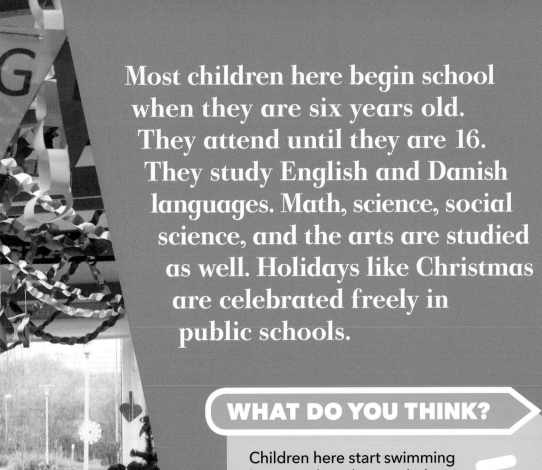

Most children here begin school when they are six years old. They attend until they are 16. They study English and Danish languages. Math, science, social science, and the arts are studied as well. Holidays like Christmas are celebrated freely in public schools.

## WHAT DO YOU THINK?

Children here start swimming lessons when they are babies. Why? Going to pools is part of the **culture**. And fishing is an important job here. Do you think swimming lessons should be required? Why or why not?

Iceland has more **hot springs** than any other country! They are warm public swimming pools. People gather at the pools. They swim and soak in the water. Some apply face masks.

Would you like to visit the land of fire and ice?

## DID YOU KNOW?

**Geothermal energy** warms homes and buildings here. How is this created? Water under Earth is heated by volcanic **magma**. The hot water enters homes and buildings through pipes.

# QUICK FACTS & TOOLS

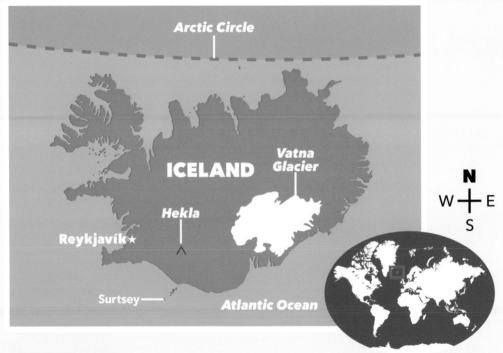

## ICELAND

**Location:** northern Europe

**Size:** 39,769 square miles (103,001 square kilometers)

**Population:** 343,518 (July 2018 estimate)

**Capital:** Reykjavík

**Type of Government:** unitary parliamentary republic

**Languages:** Icelandic, English, Nordic languages, German

**Exports:** agricultural products, fish and fish products, medical products

**Currency:** Icelandic króna

**active:** An active volcano is one that has had at least one eruption within the past 10,000 years.

**Arctic Circle:** The area surrounding the northern part of Earth.

**capital:** A city where government leaders meet.

**culture:** The ideas, customs, traditions, and ways of life of a group of people.

**export:** A product sold to different countries.

**geothermal energy:** Thermal, or heated, energy that is made and stored within Earth.

**glaciers:** Very large, slow-moving masses of ice.

**hot springs:** Natural sources of hot water that flow from the ground.

**magma:** Melted rock found beneath Earth's surface that becomes lava when it flows out of volcanoes.

**meadows:** Grassy fields, especially those used for grazing or for harvesting hay.

**prime minister:** The leader of a country.

**unity:** The state of being united or joined as a whole.

**Vikings:** Scandinavian people who invaded the coasts of Europe and explored the North American coast between the 700s and 1000s.

**volcanoes:** Mountains with openings through which molten lava, ash, and hot gases erupt.

Iceland's currency

## INDEX

## TO LEARN MORE

**Finding more information is as easy as 1, 2, 3.**

**❶ Go to www.factsurfer.com**

**❷ Enter "Iceland" into the search box.**

**❸ Click the "Surf" button to see a list of websites.**

**FACT SURFER**